Feb. 4, 2008

Migrating Animals of the Land

by Thea Feldman

Reading consultant:
Susan Nations, M.Ed.
author, literacy coach, and consultant in literacy development

Science and curriculum consultant:
Debra Voege, M.A.
science and math curriculum resource teacher

WEEKLY READER®
PUBLISHING

Please visit our web site at: www.garethstevens.com
For a free color catalog describing our list of high-quality books,
call 1-800-542-2595 (USA) or 1-800-387-3178 (Canada).

Library of Congress Cataloging-in-Publication Data available upon request from publisher.

ISBN-13: 978-0-8368-8418-0 (lib. bdg.)
ISBN-10: 0-8368-8418-3 (lib. bdg.)
ISBN-13: 978-0-8368-8423-4 (softcover)
ISBN-10: 0-8368-8423-X (softcover)

This edition first published in 2008 by
Weekly Reader® Books
An imprint of Gareth Stevens Publishing
1 Reader's Digest Road
Pleasantville, NY 10570-7000 USA

Copyright © 2008 by Gareth Stevens, Inc.

Photo credits: Cover: © Photodisc/Business & Industry, Vol.1; p.4-21: © Photodisc/Techno
Finance; cover: Martin Harvey/Corbis; p. 4: Steve and Ann Toon/Corbis; p.5: Richard Hamilton
Smith/Corbis; p.6: Digital Vision/Getty; p.8: Erwin & Peggy Bauer/Animals Animals; p.9:
Joe McDonald/Corbis; p.10: Michio Hoshino/Minden Pictures; p.11: Art Wolfe/Getty Images;
p.12: John Conrad/Corbis; p.13: George D. Lepp/Corbis; p.14: Christopher Burki/Getty Images;
p.15: Patti Murray/Animals Animals; p.18: Mitsuaki Iwago/Minden Pictures; Frans Lanting/Minden
Pictures; p.20: Craig Lovell/Corbis

Printed in the United States of America

1 2 3 4 5 6 7 8 9 11 10 09 08 07

Table of Contents

Cover and title page: African elephants stir up a lot of dust as they thunder across the African savanna.

Why Do Animals Migrate?

Would you walk a long distance for something important? Would you go on a trek no matter what the weather was like? You would if you were one of the planet's migrating land animals.

Many mammals migrate to bear their young in safe places where food is plentiful. Here, an African springbok antelope and its baby graze together.

Migration is a regular journey from one place to another. Some animals migrate to look for food. Changes in the seasons can make food scarce in an animal's **home range**. An animal's home range is the place it lives for an extended period of time. It is the place many animals return to at the end of a migration.

Some land animals migrate to find a place to reproduce and give birth. For other animals, a combination of things gets them walking down the road to survival.

Some animals migrate when human populations crowd into their home range.

5

Chapter 1

The Migration Masters

The long-distance migration record for land animals belongs to the **barren ground caribou** of Alaska and northern Canada. These deer make a round-trip annual migration that can cover more than 3,000 miles (4,800 kilometers). That is farther than the flying distance between New York City and Los Angeles! And though a jet can fly that distance in about five hours, caribou take about nine months to complete their journey.

Both male and female caribou have antlers. In most types of deer only the males have antlers.

Caribou spend cold winters below the **tree line** of the Arctic. Trees do not grow above the tree line. In summer the caribou move north to bear their young and graze on grasses and lichens near the coast.

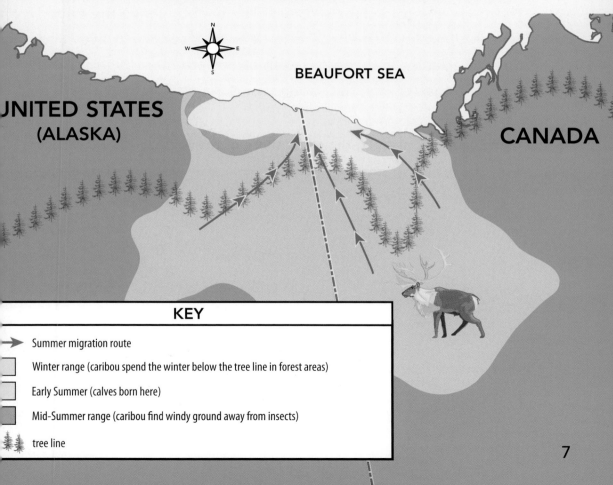

BEAUFORT SEA

UNITED STATES
(ALASKA)

CANADA

KEY

→ Summer migration route

☐ Winter range (caribou spend the winter below the tree line in forest areas)

☐ Early Summer (calves born here)

☐ Mid-Summer range (caribou find windy ground away from insects)

🌲 tree line

Caribou begin their journey when it is time for their calves to be born. Caribou **cows** migrate to the coast of Alaska from their winter feeding grounds among the trees of the **taiga**. The taiga is a cold climate forest. The caribou leave the taiga in early June for a safer place to bear their young. Wolves and other predators that can threaten calves are more plentiful in the taiga than on the flat, open plains.

Young caribou run along the rocky shore of the Arctic.

A caribou calf can walk within two hours of being born and in just days is able to travel fast enough to keep up with the herd. That is important because by mid-July the herd is on the move. The deer head north to windy hilltops free from pesky mosquitoes and full of grasses and **lichens**.

Arctic meadows are lush with low-growing plants for the caribou to graze in summer.

In the fall, caribou journey south to escape heavy snows and extremely low temperatures. Hundreds of thousands of animals travel together in a herd spreading out for hundreds of miles or kilometers. They face many dangers, including predators, drowning while crossing raging rivers, or falling through thin ice. But most arrive safely back at their winter feeding grounds.

Caribou swim in a herd across an Alaskan river on their annual migration.

Chapter 2

Winter Walkers

Mule deer, another type of North American deer, travel to find food during cold, snowy winters. They travel less than 100 miles (160 kilometers)—all downhill! Mule deer summer in the mountains, eating plants and berries. They winter in the valleys, where softer snow makes it easier to uncover **vegetation**.

A mule deer heads uphill in summer, downhill in winter.

Not all animals travel away from the cold. In fact, for the polar bear, the colder the better! Polar bears spend part of the year living on **ice floes**—large floating sheets of ice—above the Arctic Circle, hunting for a favorite food—ringed seals.

When the ice spreads in the winter, polar bears have a wider range. Many migrate south. When the ice shrinks in the spring and summer, the bears head back north. Some bears take too much time to get to the northern ice pack as it shrinks. They get stranded on land. There they eat arctic animals (including caribou!) and **forage**, or search, for berries. Then they gather at the coast in fall, waiting for the water to freeze so they can head north again.

Home on the ice! This polar bear's range is greatest when the polar sea has frozen over.

Many scientists worry that global warming is shrinking the ice pack and destroying the polar bear's natural home.

Polar bears and humans often come face to face at the edge of the ice pack. Photographers and tourists gather where the polar bears wait for the sea to freeze over.

Chapter 3

Feeding and Breeding

Army ants travel in huge **colonies** of up to 2,000,000 members! Many of these ants are only about 2/3 of an inch (1 cm) long, but a colony on the move can form a mass more than 30 feet (9 m) wide.

The fangs of some army ants can pierce skin to the bone.

These **carnivorous** (meat-eating) insects of South and Central America and Africa are nomads. They have no home range. They must keep traveling to find enough food. They eat any insect in their path, and also kill small animals such as rodents and lizards that get in their way. Army ants travel mostly at night and can kill and eat up to 100,000 insects in one foraging raid.

Army ants have killed this lizard, which wasn't able to get out of the way fast enough. The ants swarm over small reptiles and rodents, biting with their fangs.

Only the queen ant in an army ant colony reproduces, laying eggs during the colony's resting periods. The red crabs of Australia's Christmas Island, however, migrate so *each* can breed. Each November these land crabs begin an 18-day journey from their forest **burrows** to the seacoast. Each female releases up to 100,000 eggs into the sea.

When the red crabs of Christmas Island get moving, nothing gets in their way—not even a building. They just walk on through!

The eggs hatch immediately. The hatchlings, called **megalops**, spend a month in the water where they risk being eaten by manta rays and huge whale sharks. Those that survive move to shore, begin to breathe air instead of water, and make their way to the forest. There they spend most of the next two to three years underground.

Christmas Island belongs to Australia but is far from its Northwest Coast.

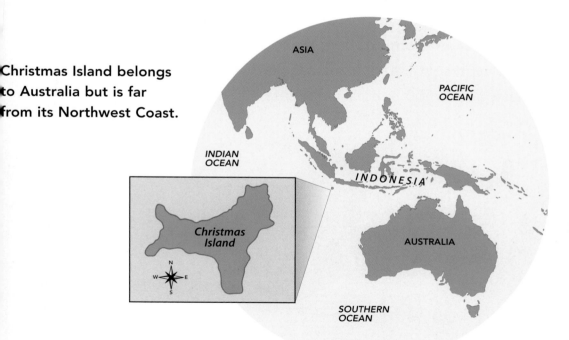

Chapter 4

Have Trunk, Will Travel

African elephants also migrate to find enough food. If they didn't, there would be nothing left to eat! Elephants spend most of their day eating. Each of the giant **herbivores**, or plant-eaters, eats more than 300 pounds (136 kg) of food a day.

An elephant herd usually has about 20 females and young males. During a migration, many smaller herds band together, and even solitary adult males join in. One migrating herd can have about 500 hungry elephants.

A herd begins its migration.

During the rainy season, elephants head south to the **savanna** where the grass is green and growing. In the dry season, the elephants migrate back north to feed on trees and bark in woodland patches along riverbanks.

Migrating elephant herds tromp through wetlands in search of food.

Spotlight: The Serengeti Migration

The world's largest and most dangerous migration takes place annually in the Serengeti, a region of savanna and woodlands in Tanzania, a country in Africa. Close to 1,500,000 wildebeest and 750,000 zebras migrate the way that elephants do, heading south to the lush savanna—a grassy plain—in the rainy season. They stay there to graze.

An enormous wildebeest herd fills the Serengeti plains.

They go back to the woodlands in the dry season. They face many dangers along the way, including the potential to be trampled by the crowd. Some animals fall prey to predators, including the deadly river crocodile. Nearly 500,000 wildebeest calves are born on the savanna and are ready to migrate when the herd returns north.

The Great Migration of the Serengeti

UGANDA

KENYA

ÁFRICA

Lake Victoria

September–October
Animals are on their home range in Kenya.

November–December
Animals begin to move south into Tanzania looking for water.

Serengeti Plains

April–August
Animals move west and north, back towards Kenya.

January–March
Animals graze on the grassy plains. Many animals have their babies.

TANZANIA

KEY

Home range

Trip south

Trip home

N
W   E
S

21

Glossary

Arctic Circle—the line that marks the region surrounding the North Pole

burrow—a small, snug living space an animal digs into the ground

carnivorous—meat-eating

colony—a group of animals, such as ants, that live together and depend on one another

cow—a female of a large animal species

forage—to go from place to place in search of food

hatchling—a newly hatched bird, fish, amphibian, or reptile

herbivore—a plant eater

home range—the place an animal lives for an extended period of time

ice floe—a sheet of floating ice

lichen—a gray, green, or yellow plant-like organism that grows on a flat rock or another flat surface

megalops—a red crab that is less than one month old

migration—a regular journey from one place to another to find food, to mate, or to find a better climate

nomad—an animal that moves from place to place in search of food

plain—a large area of flat, grassy land without trees

predator—an animal that kills other animals for food

savanna—a flat grassland area with few trees

taiga—a forest in a cold climate

vegetation—the plants that grow in a place

For More Information

Books

The Extraordinary Travels of Animals on Land; They Walk the Earth. Seymour Simon. (Browndeer Press/Harcourt).

The Journey, Stories of Migration. Cynthia Rylant. (Scholastic).

Serengeti Migration: Africa's Animals on the Move. Lisa Lindblad. (Hyperion).

Nature's Minibeasts: Army Ants. Clint Twist. (Gareth Stevens).

Web Sites

Caribou Migration
http:arctic.fws.gov/carcon.htm

Polar Bear Migration
http:www.adfg.state.ak.us/pubs/notebook/marine/polarbea.php

The Red Crabs of Christmas island
http:www.deh.gov.au/parks/christmas/fauna/redcrabs.html

23

Index

About the Author

Thea Feldman has been writing and editing children's books for over 25 years. She also writes about animals and the environment for a global conservation organization. Thea lives in New York City, where she watches the daily migration of her cat, Zoe, from the couch to the kitchen.